BOSTON COMMON PRESS
Brookline, Massachusetts

1997

Boston Common Press
17 Station Street
Brookline, Massachusetts 02146

ISBN 0-936184-20-5
Library of Congress Cataloging-in-Publication Data
The Editors of *Cook's Illustrated*
    How to make pizza: An illustrated step-by-step guide to perfect thin-crust, deep-dish, and grilled pizza/The Editors of *Cook's Illustrated*
1st ed.

    Includes 38 recipes and 39 illustrations
    ISBN 0-936184-20-5 (hardback): $14.95
    I. Cooking. I. Title
1997

Manufactured in the United States of America

Distributed by Boston Common Press, 17 Station Street, Brookline, MA 02146.

Cover and text design by Amy Klee
Recipe development by Melissa Hamilton
Series Editor: Jack Bishop

HOW TO MAKE PIZZA

An illustrated step-by-step guide to
thin-crust, deep-dish, and grilled pizza.

THE COOK'S ILLUSTRATED LIBRARY

Illustrations by John Burgoyne

CONTENTS

introduction

ß

OOK'S ILLUSTRATED IS KNOWN FOR FINDING the ultimate recipe for a particular dish, whether it be brownies or crown roast of pork. And certainly, we have pursued the same rigorous testing in this book, whether it be a basic pizza dough, thin-crust pizza, deep-dish or even grilled. But I have found over the years that pizza is a bit of a contradiction. It's a simple, workhorse recipe suitable for weekday dinners, yet it does require advance preparation: The dough must be made, allowed to rise, topped, and then baked.

So this book endeavors to solve the problem of how to put pizza on the table from start to finish in less than 90 minutes. By using rapid rise yeast and a preheated oven as a proofing box, you can now make pizza on a Tuesday night with no advance planning and only a modest amount of labor. Of course, we also developed a 24-hour dough recipe which can be started the night before, refrigerated overnight, and then left to stand at room temperature for up to 8 hours.

Both methods work well especially when paired with our no-cook tomato sauce, which further simplifies the process.

In addition to thin-crust pizza dough, we developed recipes for deep-dish and grilled pizza, the latter being an excellent accompaniment to any grilled dinner. We also provide variations on the basic dough recipe, some flavored with garlic, other with semolina, cornmeal, or whole wheat flour.

We also provide plenty of in-depth techniques and illustrations. The basic dough recipe can be made by hand, in just seconds in a food processor, and in a few minutes in a standing mixer. We hope that you find this to be a useful guide to one of the most useful recipes in any home cook's repertoire.

We have also published *How to Make a Pie, How to Make an American Layer Cake, How to Stir-Fry, and How to Make Ice Cream*, and many other titles in this series will soon be available. To order other books, call us at 800-611-0759. We are also the editors and publishers of *Cook's Illustrated*, a bimonthly publication about American home cooking. For a free trial copy of *Cook's Illustrated*, call 800-526-8442.

Sincerely,

Christopher Kimball
Editor and Publisher
Cook's Illustrated

chapter one

❦

PIZZA BASICS

IZZA MAY BE CALLED FAST FOOD, BUT YOU'VE got plenty to do before you can get it in the oven. There's dough to knead, let rise, and stretch; tomato sauce to make; cheese to grate; and toppings to prepare. Little wonder so many people have surrendered to shredded mozzarella and premade dough.

The problem, of course, is that these shortcuts come with a price: an extreme drop in quality. Homemade pizza is superb. Our goal was to find as many shortcuts as possible to streamline the preparation of the various components.

We also wanted to develop a variety of recipes for different kinds of pizza. Although pizza has its origins in Italy, it

8

has become a thoroughly American dish, with many regional differences. Chapter three focuses on thin-crust pizza, which is king in New York and other eastern pizza capitals; Chapter four covers deep-dish or Chicago-style pan pizza; and Chapter five is devoted to grilled pizza, first popularized in California, but now common throughout the country.

While these three kinds of pizza all rely on similar doughs and sauces, the techniques for shaping and baking each style of pizza are really quite different. Listed below are a number of pieces of equipment you will use throughout this book.

TOOLS OF THE TRADE

▪ INSTANT READ THERMOMETER. Successful dough starts with water at the proper temperature. An instant-read thermometer, preferably a digital one with a quick response time and easy-to-read display, guarantees accurate readings.

▪ FOOD PROCESSOR. Although doughs can be kneaded by hand or in a standing mixer, we find that a large-capacity food processor does the job quickly and efficiently. When choosing a food processor, look for a model with an eleven-cup workbowl (smaller models cannot knead a dough with four cups of flour) and a heavy base (at least ten pounds) that will prevent the food processor from jumping across the counter as the blade spins through the thick dough.

■ BAKING SHEETS AND PEELS. For thin-crust pizza, we like to transfer stretched dough to a peel that has been dusted with semolina. The long handle on the peel makes it easy to slide the dough onto tiles or a stone in a hot oven. Although a rimless metal baking sheet can be used in this fashion, the lack of a handle puts your hands that much closer to the oven heat.

When shopping for a pizza peel, note that there are two choices. Aluminum peels with heat-resistant wooden handles are probably the better bet because they can be washed and cleaned easily. Wooden peels can mildew when washed so it's best just to wipe them clean. Either way, make sure your peel measures at least sixteen inches across.

For grilled pizzas, we like to put stretched dough rounds on a rimless baking sheet or aluminum peel that has been dusted with flour. We do not feel comfortable placing a wooden peel so close to an open fire.

■ BAKING TILES OR STONE. If you like thin-crust pizza, we recommend you invest $15 or $20 to line the bottom rack of your oven with unglazed quarry tiles made of terra-cotta. These porous tiles come in six-inch squares and can be cut at a tile store to fit your oven rack perfectly. Look for one-half-inch-thick tiles.

A large rectangular pizza stone is also a good option.

The chief drawback here is size. In most home ovens, you can fit two medium pizzas on a tile-lined rack. However, most pizza stones can only fit one pizza at a time. If using a stone, take care when sliding the pizza into the oven. You don't want part of the pizza to hang off the stone, dumping toppings onto the oven floor.

DEEP-DISH PIZZA PAN. If you like deep-dish pizza, we recommend buying a fourteen-inch round metal pan that is two inches deep. We tested shiny and dark pans, and both browned the crust equally well.

LONG-HANDLED GRILL TOOLS. Grilling pizza over a hot fire can be tricky. Tongs with long, heat-resistant handles are essential. A fork (for pricking any bubbles that form in the crust) and brush (for painting on oil) with long, heat-resistant handles are also worth owning.

PIZZA WHEEL. A pizza wheel will quickly turn a piping hot pizza into wedges or slices ready to eat. Although a pizza wheel looks like a pastry wheel, it should have a much stronger handle that is offset from a much stronger blade to provide the leverage necessary to cut through thick crusts. Make sure the cutting wheel is large enough (four inches is good) to get through a deep-dish pizza.

11

chapter two

⋹

DOUGHS AND SAUCES

THE DOUGH IS PROBABLY THE TRICKIEST part of pizza making at home. While pizza dough is nothing more than bread dough with oil added for softness and suppleness, we found in our testing that minor changes in the ingredients list can yield dramatically different results.

Our goal in testing was threefold. We wanted to develop a recipe that was simple to put together; the dough had to be easy to shape and stretch; and the crust needed to bake up properly: crisp and chewy (but not tough and leathery) for thin-crust and grilled pizzas; tender and chewy for deep-dish pizza, with a lighter, more open crumb.

After some initial tests, it was clear that bread flour delivers the best texture for thin-crust and grilled pizzas. Bread flour makes pizza crust that is chewy and crisp. Unbleached all-purpose flour could be used in a pinch, but the resulting crust is less crisp.

When it comes to deep-dish pizza, we prefer all-purpose flour. We found that unbleached all-purpose flour, with its lower protein content, makes the dough softer with a more breadlike chew than the same dough made with bread flour. To add softness and suppleness, we more than doubled the amount of oil in this dough.

The second key to perfect crust is water. We found that using more water makes the dough softer and more elastic. It stretches more easily than a stiffer, harder dough with less water. We prefer to jump-start the yeast in a little warm water for five minutes. We then add more room-temperature water and oil.

When it comes to combining the dry ingredients (flour and salt) with the wet ingredients, the food processor is our first choice. The liquid gets evenly incorporated into the dry ingredients, and the blade kneads the dough in just thirty seconds. Of course, the dough can be kneaded by hand or with a standing mixer. If making the dough by hand, resist the temptation to add a lot of flour as you knead.

It is possible to flavor pizza dough (we offer several variations) or to change the rising time by using less yeast and/or refrigerating the dough. This way, dough can be made the night before or in the morning and ready when you need it for dinner. We also have developed a quick dough for thin-crust pizza that is ready for the oven in one hour. Keep the following tips in mind when making pizza dough.

CHOOSE THE RIGHT FLOUR. Bread flour makes crisp crusts and is the perfect choice for thin-crust pizza or grilled pizza, which is also fairly thin. All-purpose flour makes a soft, chewy, more breadlike crust, ideal for deep-dish pizza.

CHANGE THE FLAVOR. For a change of pace, it is easy to alter the flavor of the crust. Add a little semolina or corn-meal to the dough. The results are similar although the semolina makes a slightly lighter and crisper crust. Whole wheat flour gives pizza crust a hearty flavor but may slow down the rising time a bit. Garlic and herbs will add flavor to any dough but are especially welcome in a grilled pizza because the toppings are so light.

KEEP IT COVERED. Use plastic wrap to cover the oiled bowl with the rising dough. The tight seal offered by plastic wrap keeps the dough moist and protects it from drafts. We reserve the traditional damp cloth for when the dough has been divided into balls and is waiting to be stretched out.

■■ LET IT RISE AT YOUR OWN PACE. Decreasing the yeast slows down the rising time, making it possible to mix dough in the morning and then shape it at dinnertime. You may also chill the dough to retard development of the yeast, allowing the dough to be refrigerated overnight and then to rise during the day and be shaped at dinnertime.

■■ GIVE IT A REST. In order to stretch dough to its maximum diameter, let it rest one or two times during the shaping process. Once you feel some resistance from the dough, cover it with a damp cloth, and wait five minutes before going at it again. We find that fingertips and hands do a better job of stretching dough than a rolling pin, which presses out air from the risen dough and makes it tough. Our low-tech method is also superior to flipping dough into the air and other silly directions that may work in a pizza parlor but can cause disaster at home.

■■ FREEZE LEFTOVER DOUGH. Even if baking just one medium pizza, make a full dough recipe. After the dough has risen and been divided, place the extra dough in an airtight container and freeze it for up to several weeks. Defrost and stretch the dough when desired.

♛

Master Recipe

Basic Pizza Dough

➤ NOTE: *We find that the food processor is the best tool for making pizza dough. However, you can knead this dough by hand or in a standing mixer (see notes below). See figures 1–8, page 20, for more information on the dough-making process. Note that the flavor variations on page 19 can be used interchangeably with the time and kneading variations. For instance, you can make 8-Hour Cornmeal Pizza Dough and knead it by hand if you like.*

½	cup warm water, at about 105 degrees
1	envelope (2¼ teaspoons) active dry yeast
1¼	cups water, at room temperature
2	tablespoons olive oil
4	cups bread flour, plus extra for dusting hands and work surfaces
1½	teaspoons salt
	Vegetable oil or spray for oiling bowl

16

Master Instructions

1. Measure warm water into 2-cup measuring cup. Sprinkle in yeast; let stand until yeast dissolves and swells, about 5 minutes. Add room-temperature water and oil; stir to combine.

2. Pulse flour and salt in workbowl of large food processor fitted with steel blade to combine. Continue pulsing while pouring liquid ingredients (holding back a few tablespoons) through feed tube. If dough does not readily form into ball, add remaining liquid, and continue to pulse until ball forms. Process until dough is smooth and elastic, about 30 seconds longer.

3. Dough will be a bit tacky, so use rubber spatula to turn out dough onto lightly floured work surface; knead by hand with a few strokes to form smooth, round ball. Put dough into deep oiled bowl and cover with plastic wrap. Let rise until doubled in size, about 2 hours. Punch dough down and turn out onto lightly floured work surface. Divide, if necessary, and shape as directed in master recipe for thin-crust, deep-dish, or grilled pizza.

▐▌ VARIATIONS:

To Knead by Hand: Instead of step 2, combine salt and half of flour in deep bowl. Add liquid ingredients and use wooden spoon to combine. Add remaining flour, stirring until cohesive mass forms. Turn dough out onto lightly floured work surface and knead until smooth and elastic, 7 to 8 minutes. Use as little dusting flour as possible while kneading. Form dough into ball, put it into deep oiled bowl, cover with plastic wrap, and proceed with recipe.

To Knead in a Standing Mixer: Instead of step 2, place flour and salt in deep bowl of standing mixer. With paddle attachment, briefly combine dry ingredients on low speed. Slowly add liquid ingredients and continue to mix on low speed until cohesive mass forms. Stop mixer and replace paddle with dough hook. Knead until dough is smooth and elastic, about 5 minutes. Form dough into ball, put it into deep oiled bowl, cover with plastic wrap, and proceed with recipe.

24-Hour Pizza Dough

Decrease yeast to ½ teaspoon. Let covered dough rise in refrigerator for up to 16 hours. Finish rising at room temperature until doubled in size, 6 to 8 hours.

8-Hour Pizza Dough

Decrease yeast to ½ teaspoon. Let covered dough rise at

cool room temperature (about 68 degrees) until doubled in size, about 8 hours.

Semolina Pizza Dough

Decrease room-temperature water to 1 cup and replace ¾ cup bread flour with equal amount of semolina.

Cornmeal Pizza Dough

Replace ¾ cup bread flour with equal amount of cornmeal.

Whole Wheat Pizza Dough

Replace 2 cups bread flour with equal amount of whole wheat flour. Dough may require an extra 30 minutes to double in size while rising.

Garlic-Herb Pizza Dough

Heat 2 tablespoons olive oil in small skillet. Add 4 medium minced garlic cloves and 1 teaspoon minced fresh thyme, oregano, or rosemary leaves. Sauté until garlic is golden, 2 to 3 minutes. Cool and use in place of oil in master recipe.

Deep-Dish Pizza Dough

Reduce yeast to 1½ teaspoons, room-temperature water to ¾ cup, and salt to 1¼ teaspoons; use 3 cups unbleached all-purpose flour in place of the 4 cups of bread flour; and increase oil to 3 tablespoons. Knead dough in food processor or by hand, not in standing mixer.

Figure 1.
Measure ½ cup of warm water at about 105 degrees into a
2-cup measuring cup. Sprinkle the yeast over the water and
let it stand until swelled, about 5 minutes. Add enough
room-temperature water to equal 1¾ cups and then add the oil.

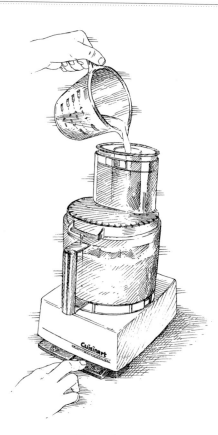

Figure 2.
The food processor is the easiest place to make pizza dough.
Pulse the flour and salt to combine them. Then, pour the liquid
ingredients through the feed tube while continuing to pulse.

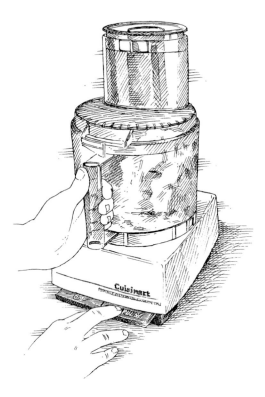

Figure 3.
Once the dough comes together, process it until it is smooth and
elastic, about 30 seconds.

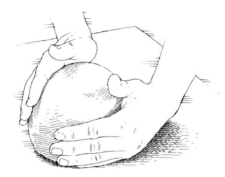

Figure 4.
Turn the dough onto a lightly floured work surface and shape it
into a smooth, round ball.

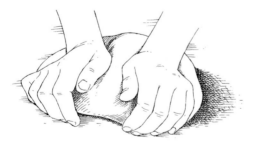

Figure 5.
If kneading dough by hand, don't worry about overworking the
dough. You can't be too rough. Use your palms for maximum
leverage against the dough.

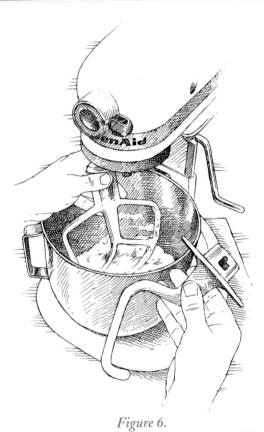

Figure 6.
If kneading dough in a standing mixer, use the paddle
attachment to combine the dry and wet ingredients.
When the dough forms a cohesive mass, stop the mixer and
switch to the dough hook for kneading.

24

Figure 7.
Plastic wrap forms a tighter seal than a damp towel and keeps
the dough moister. Place the kneaded dough into a deep oiled
bowl and cover the bowl tightly with the wrap.

Figure 8.
After the dough has doubled in size (about 2 hours), deflate it by
punching down on the dough with your fist. Divide, if necessary,
and shape the punched-down dough as directed in the master
recipes for thin-crust, deep-dish, or grilled pizza.

75-Minute Pizza-Dough

➤ NOTE: *Although this quick dough does not quite have the same texture as our master recipe dough, it can be made after coming home from work to make thin-crust pizza. Rapid-rise yeast makes it possible to serve pizza in a little more than an hour after walking into the kitchen. The sugar also speeds up the rising process as does putting the dough into a warm oven. Although we prefer bread flour because it delivers a crisper crust, you may use all-purpose flour.*

1½	cups warm water, at about 105 degrees
1	envelope (2¼ teaspoons) rapid-rise dry yeast
1	tablespoon sugar
2	tablespoons olive oil
4	cups bread or all-purpose flour, plus extra for dusting hands and work surfaces
1½	teaspoons salt
	Vegetable oil or spray for oiling bowl

∷ INSTRUCTIONS:

1. Set oven to 200 degrees for 10 minutes, then turn oven off.

2. Meanwhile, pour water into workbowl of large food processor. Sprinkle yeast and sugar over water and pulse twice. Add oil, flour, and salt and process until mixture forms cohesive mass. Dough should be soft and just a bit tacky. (If it is very sticky, add 2 tablespoons flour and pulse

2 6

briefly. If it is stiff and tight, add 1 tablespoon water and pulse briefly.) Process another 30 seconds.

3. Dough will be a bit tacky, so use rubber spatula to turn out dough onto lightly floured work surface; knead by hand with a few strokes to form smooth, round ball.

4. Put dough into deep lightly oiled bowl and cover with plastic wrap. Place in warm oven. Let rise for 40 minutes or until doubled. Remove from oven, punch dough down, and turn out onto lightly floured work surface. Divide and shape as directed in Master Recipe for Thin-Crust Pizza.

No-Cook Tomato Sauce

➤ NOTE: *We found that the oven heat "cooks" the tomato sauce when making thin-crust pizza. Simply combine canned crushed tomatoes, oil, garlic, salt, and pepper and then spread the mixture on the dough as needed. When shopping for crushed tomatoes, look for a brand that lists tomatoes, not tomato puree, as the first ingredient. In our testing, we have found that Muir Glen and Progresso are both excellent products. This recipe yields about 3 cups of sauce. Note that because of the lower oven temperature, no-cook tomato sauce will make deep-dish pizza soggy; follow the Thick Tomato Sauce variation at right when making deep-dish pizza.*

- 1   **28-ounce can crushed tomatoes**
- 2   **tablespoons extra-virgin olive oil**
- 2   **large garlic cloves, minced**
       Salt and ground black pepper

INSTRUCTIONS:

Combine tomatoes, oil, garlic, and salt and pepper to taste in medium bowl. Set aside at room temperature for up to several hours. (Sauce may be refrigerated in airtight container for 3 days.)

:: **VARIATIONS:**

Spicy No-Cook Tomato Sauce
Add 1 teaspoon hot red pepper flakes.

No-Cook Tomato Sauce with Basil
Add 2 tablespoons minced fresh basil leaves.

Thick Tomato Sauce
Place all ingredients in medium saucepan and simmer until thick and reduced to 2½ cups, about 20 minutes.

chapter three

3

THIN-CRUST PIZZA

NLESS YOU BUILD A BRICK OVEN IN YOUR kitchen, it's not possible to duplicate thin pizzeria-style pies at home. Commercial pizza ovens can reach 800 degrees; home ovens just can't compete. That said, homemade thin-crust pizza is delicious, if different, from the pies you get when you eat out. The crust is chewier, crisper, and not nearly as greasy.

While American pizza parlors weigh down their crusts with pounds of toppings, we prefer to follow the Italian method and use a restrained hand when topping a thin-crust pizza. This is partly out of necessity (without the extreme heat of a commercial oven, crusts with so much cheese and sauce will be soggy) and partly because we like pizzas this way. After all, you are making homemade bread, and pizza should be about the crust as well as the cheese and sauce.

In our testing, we found that baking thin-crust pizza on tiles or a pizza stone is a must. Thin crusts baked on a pizza screen (a perforated pan) or baking sheet will not be as crisp and chewy. (*See* Tools of the Trade, page 9, for more information on buying these items.)

Our testing revealed that an oven temperature of 450 degrees is your best bet. We could not detect any extra crispness in a pizza cooked in a 500-degree oven. What we did notice was a fair amount of smoke in our kitchen. If your oven works well at 500 degrees without smoking, feel free to bake pizzas at this temperature; you will shave a minute or two off the cooking time.

This chapter starts with some simple pizzas that are baked plain and then topped with herb oil, pesto, or cheeses. Pizzas with raw toppings such as fresh tomatoes, prosciutto, and arugula are next, followed by more complex pizzas with cooked meat, vegetable, and seafood toppings.

Keep the following tips in mind when making thin-crust pizza.

⠿ DUST PEEL WITH SEMOLINA. With its fine, sandy texture, semolina keeps pizza dough from sticking to peels. Cornmeal can be used, but we find that its coarser texture can make the bottom of the crust a bit gritty.

⠿ ADD MELTING CHEESES AT END OF BAKING. To keep soft cheeses like mozzarella moist and lush, we prefer to add them toward the end of the baking time. When added earlier, mozzarella tends to shrivel up and dry out. Adding it later also gets more impact from less cheese, keeping the fat content to a minimum. Grating cheeses, like Parmesan, may be added at the start or near the end of baking as desired.

⠿ BAKING TIMES WILL VARY. Depending on your oven, the type of stone or tiles used, the size of the dough round, and the amount of topping, thin-crust pizzas may be done in as little as five or six minutes or may take as long as twelve minutes. Larger pies with heavier or juicier toppings may sometimes require closer to fifteen minutes. Don't pull a pizza out of the oven until the edge of the crust is golden brown and the toppings are sizzling.

♛

Master Recipe

Thin Crust Pizza

➤ **NOTE:** *Any of the variations on basic pizza dough (except the deep-dish dough) may be used to make thin-crust pizza. See figures 9–19, page 36, for more information on stretching and baking thin-crust pizza. This recipe makes two large, four medium, or eight individual pies. Remember to preheat the oven (and stone, if using one) for at least thirty minutes.*

1   recipe **Basic Pizza Dough** (*see* page 16)
     or **75-Minute Pizza Dough**
     (*see* page 26)
     Flour for dusting hands and work surfaces
     Semolina or cornmeal for dusting peel
     Olive oil for brushing on dough
     Toppings of choice (*see* following recipes)

♔
Master Instructions
Thin Crust Pizza

1. Prepare dough as directed in dough recipe. Preheat oven at 450 degrees, placing pizza stone on rack in lower third of oven if not already lined with tiles, for 30 minutes. Turn punched-down dough out onto lightly floured work surface. Use chef's knife or dough scraper to halve, quarter, or cut dough into eighths, depending on number and size of pizzas desired. Form each piece into ball and cover with damp cloth. Let dough relax at least 5 minutes but not more than 30 minutes.

2. Working with one piece of dough at a time and keeping others covered, flatten ball into disk using palms of hands. Starting at center and working outward, use fingertips to press dough to about ½-inch thick. Use one hand to hold dough in place and other hand to stretch dough outward; rotate dough quarter turn and stretch again. Repeat turning and stretching until dough will not stretch any further. Let dough relax 5 minutes; continue stretching until it reaches correct diameter. Dough should be about ¼ inch thick.

Master Instructions

(For large pizzas, let dough relax another 5 minutes and stretch again.) Use palm to flatten edge of dough. Transfer dough rounds to pizza peel that has been lightly dusted with semolina or cornmeal.

3. Brush dough rounds very lightly with oil and then add toppings. Cook topped pizzas in preheated oven until edges of crusts are golden brown, 5 to 12 minutes depending on size of pizzas. Add cheese if using and continue baking until melted, 2 to 3 minutes. Remove pizzas from oven, cut into wedges, and serve immediately.

Figure 9.
Thin-crust pizza must be baked on tiles or a pizza stone.
You may line a rack in the lower third of your oven with quarry
tiles. If using a pizza stone, place it on the rack before turning
the oven on. Either way, preheat the oven for 30 minutes so that
the tiles or stone becomes very hot.

36

Figure 10.
Use a chef's knife or dough scraper to divide the risen and
punched-down dough into two, four, or eight pieces.
A single dough recipe will make two 14-inch pizzas,
four 12-inch pizzas, or eight 8-inch pies.

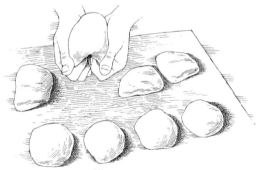

Figure 11.
Form each piece of dough into a smooth, round ball and cover
it with a damp cloth. Let the dough relax for at least 5 minutes
but no more than 30 minutes.

Figure 12.
Working with one ball of dough at a time and keeping the
others covered, flatten the dough ball into a disk using the
palms of your hands.

Figure 13.
Starting at the center of the disk and working outward,
use your fingertips to press the dough to about ½-inch thick.

3 8

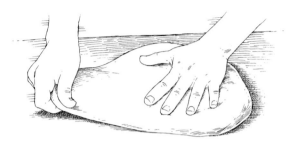

Figure 14.

Use one hand to hold the dough in place and the other hand to stretch the dough outward. Rotate the dough a quarter turn and stretch it again. Repeat the turning and stretching until the dough will not stretch any further. Let the dough relax for 5 minutes, then continue stretching until it reaches the correct diameter. For large pizzas, you may need to let the dough rest again before it will stretch to the desired size.

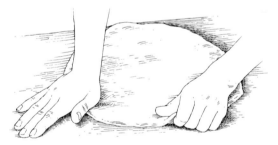

Figure 15.

Use your palm to press down and flatten the thick edge of the dough.

Figure 16.
Carefully lift the dough round and transfer it to a peel dusted
with semolina or cornmeal.

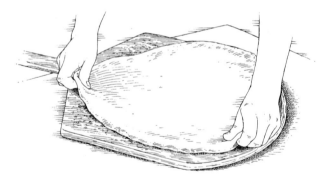

Figure 17.
If the dough loses its round shape, adjust it on the peel to
return it to the original shape.

Figure 18.

*Brush the entire dough round with a little olive oil. Add the top-
pings. To make it easier to hold pizza slices when eating, leave a
½-inch border around the edges of the dough uncovered.*

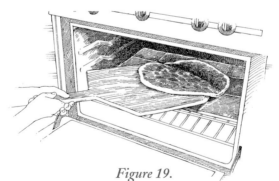

Figure 19.

*Use a quick jerking action to slide the topped dough off the peel and
onto the hot tiles or stone. Make sure that the pizza lands far enough
back so that the front edge does not hang off the tiles or stone.*

41

Pizza Bianca with Garlic and Rosemary

➤ **NOTE:** *This simple pizza is best as a snack or bread accompaniment to dinner. Pizza bianca translates as "white pizza" and refers to the fact that there are no tomatoes, just garlic, oil, rosemary, and salt, in this recipe.*

1	recipe Thin-Crust Pizza (*see* page 33)
¼	cup extra-virgin olive oil, plus extra for brushing on stretched dough
6	medium garlic cloves, minced
4	teaspoons minced fresh rosemary leaves
	Salt and ground black pepper

INSTRUCTIONS:

1. Prepare dough rounds as directed in master recipe through step 2.

2. While preparing dough, combine ¼ cup oil, garlic, rosemary, and salt and pepper to taste in small bowl. Set herb oil aside.

3. Brush plain olive oil evenly over each stretched dough round. Prick each round all over with fork (*see* figure 20).

4. Bake until crusts begin to brown in spots, 5 to 10 minutes. Remove crusts from oven and brush with herb oil.

Continue baking 1 to 2 minutes. Remove pizzas from oven, cut into wedges, and serve immediately.

VARIATION:

Lemon–Sea Salt Pizza

Brush each dough round with plain olive oil. Arrange 2 lemons sliced paper-thin over rounds, leaving ½-inch border around edges uncovered, and sprinkle with coarse sea salt to taste. Bake until golden, 5 to 10 minutes. Brush herb oil over lemon slices and continue baking 1 to 2 minutes.

Figure 20.
When pizza dough is topped with just oil, it can bubble up as it bakes. To prevent this, prick the dough all over with a fork before it goes into the oven. If bubbles form during baking, prick them before they become too large.

Pesto Pizza

➤ **NOTE**: *The crust is baked naked for this pizza and then spread with pesto just before serving. As with the pizza bianca, it is necessary to prick the dough with a fork before baking to prevent the formation of bubbles (see figure 20, page 43). You may substitute two-thirds cup of any favorite pesto sauce in this recipe.*

1	recipe Thin-Crust Pizza (*see* page 33)
2	cups tightly packed fresh basil leaves
2	medium garlic cloves, peeled
2	tablespoons pine nuts or walnuts
½	cup extra-virgin olive oil, plus extra for brushing on stretched dough
½	cup grated Parmesan cheese
	Salt and ground black pepper

INSTRUCTIONS:

1. Prepare dough rounds as directed in master recipe through step 2.

2. While preparing dough, place basil, garlic, and nuts in workbowl of food processor. Process, scraping down sides of bowl as needed, until ingredients are finely chopped. With motor running, add ½ cup oil in steady stream through feed tube and process until smooth. Scrape sauce into bowl. Stir in cheese and salt and pepper to taste. Cover and set sauce aside.

3. Brush oil evenly over each stretched dough round. Prick each dough round all over with fork (see figure 20, page 43). Bake until crusts begin to brown in spots, 5 to 10 minutes.

4. Remove crusts from oven and spread evenly with pesto, leaving ½-inch border around edges uncovered. Cut into wedges and serve immediately.

Classic Tomato Pizza
with Mozzarella and Basil

➤ **NOTE:** *Ripe tomatoes will make all the difference here. It's imperative that excess moisture be removed from the tomatoes (see figure 23, page 48). If you don't mind the skins, don't bother peeling the tomatoes.*

1	**recipe Thin-Crust Pizza (*see* page 33)**
2	**tablespoons extra-virgin olive oil, plus extra for brushing on stretched dough**
4	**medium ripe tomatoes (about 1½ pounds), peeled if desired (*see* figures 21 and 22), seeded (*see* figure 23, page 48), and chopped**
	Salt and ground black pepper
¼	**cup shredded fresh basil leaves**
4	**ounces mozzarella cheese, shredded (about 1 cup)**
¼	**cup grated Parmesan or Pecorino Romano cheese**

⁞ INSTRUCTIONS:

1. Prepare dough rounds as directed in master recipe through step 2.

2. Brush oil evenly over each stretched dough round. Arrange portion of tomatoes over each dough round, leaving ½-inch border around edges uncovered. Season with salt and pepper to taste and scatter portion of basil over tomatoes. Drizzle with 2 tablespoons oil.

3. Bake until edges of crusts start to brown, 6 to 12 minutes. Sprinkle with cheeses and continue baking until cheeses melt, 2 to 3 minutes more. Remove pizzas from oven, cut into wedges, and serve immediately.

Figure 21.
To remove the skins from ripe tomatoes, drop the tomatoes into a saucepan filled with simmering water. After 15 seconds, use a slotted spoon to retrieve the tomatoes.

47

Figure 22.
When the tomatoes cool a bit, use a sharp paring knife to peel
away the skins.

Figure 23.
Core and cut the tomatoes in half crosswise. Squeeze the seeds out
into a bowl. Chop and reserve the tomatoes

Pepperoni Pizza

➤ NOTE: *This classic pizzeria favorite is especially easy to pre-pare because the pepperoni cooks right in the oven with the pizza.*

1	recipe Thin-Crust Pizza (*see* page 33)
	Olive oil for brushing on stretched dough
1½	cups No-Cook Tomato Sauce (*see* page 28)
8	ounces pepperoni, peeled and sliced thin
4	ounces mozzarella cheese, shredded (about 1 cup)
¼	cup grated Parmesan cheese

INSTRUCTIONS:

1. Prepare dough rounds as directed in master recipe through step 2.

2. Brush oil evenly over each stretched dough round. Spread portion of tomato sauce over each dough round, leaving ½-inch border around edges uncovered. Scatter some pepperoni slices over sauce onto each dough round.

3. Bake until edges of crusts start to brown, 6 to 12 minutes. Sprinkle with cheeses and continue baking until cheeses melt, 2 to 3 minutes more. Remove pizzas from oven, cut into wedges, and serve immediately.

49

Fresh Tomato Pizza
with Arugula and Prosciutto

➤ **NOTE:** *The arugula for this pizza is tossed with a little oil to keep it moist, then sprinkled over the baked pizza as soon as it comes out of the oven. The heat from the pizza wilts the arugula without causing it to dry out. Because these topping ingredients are not precooked, this pizza is especially easy to prepare.*

1   recipe Thin-Crust Pizza (*see* page 33)

2   tablespoons extra-virgin olive oil, plus extra for brushing on stretched dough

3   medium ripe tomatoes (about 1 pound), cored and sliced crosswise into thin rounds
      Salt and ground black pepper

4   ounces thin-sliced prosciutto (about 8 slices)

4   ounces mozzarella cheese, shredded (about 1 cup)

2   cups stemmed arugula leaves, washed and thoroughly dried

INSTRUCTIONS:

1. Prepare dough rounds as directed in master recipe through step 2.

2. Brush oil evenly over each stretched dough round. Arrange portion of tomatoes in concentric circles over each

50

dough round, leaving ½-inch border around edges uncovered. Season with salt and pepper to taste and drizzle with 4 teaspoons oil.

3. Bake until edges of crusts start to brown, 6 to 12 minutes. Lay prosciutto slices over tomatoes and sprinkle with cheese. Continue baking until cheese melts, 2 to 3 minutes more.

4. Toss arugula with remaining 2 teaspoons oil. Remove pizzas from oven and top each with portion of arugula. Cut pizzas into wedges and serve immediately.

Caramelized Onion Pizza with Oil-Cured Olives and Parmesan

➤ NOTE: *Although these pizzas are substantial enough for dinner, they are particularly good as an hors d'oeuvre when cooked and then cut into small pieces.*

1	recipe Thin-Crust Pizza (*see* page 33)
2	tablespoons olive oil, plus extra for brushing on stretched dough
2	medium yellow onions, halved and sliced thin
1	teaspoon fresh thyme leaves
	Salt and ground black pepper
1½	cups No-Cook Tomato Sauce (*see* page 28)
¼	cup pitted and quartered oil-cured black olives
6	anchovies, chopped coarse (optional)
¼	cup grated Parmesan cheese

▓ INSTRUCTIONS:

1. Prepare dough rounds as directed in master recipe through step 2.

2. While preparing dough, heat 2 tablespoons oil in large skillet set over medium-high heat. Add onions and sauté until softened and somewhat caramelized, about 10 minutes. Stir in thyme; season with salt and pepper to taste. Set onions aside.

3. Brush oil evenly over each stretched dough round. Spread portion of tomato sauce over each dough round, leaving ½-inch border around edges uncovered. Scatter portion of onions over sauce onto each dough round. Sprinkle with olives and optional anchovies.

4. Bake until edges of crusts start to brown, 6 to 12 minutes. Sprinkle with cheese and continue baking until cheese melts, 2 to 3 minutes more. Remove pizzas from oven, cut into wedges, and serve immediately.

Sausage and Bell Pepper Pizza with Basil and Mozzarella

➤ **NOTE:** *If bulk sausage is not available, buy link sausage, remove the meat from the casings, and then break it into bite-size pieces. See figures 24 and 25, page 56, for more information.*

1	recipe Thin-Crust Pizza (*see* page 33)
¾	pound bulk sweet Italian sausage, broken into bite-size pieces
1½	teaspoons olive oil (approximately), plus extra for brushing on stretched dough
1	red or yellow bell pepper, cored, halved, seeded, and cut into thin strips
	Salt and ground black pepper
1½	cups No-Cook Tomato Sauce with Basil (*see* page 29)
4	ounces mozzarella cheese, shredded (about 1 cup)

:: INSTRUCTIONS:

1. Prepare dough rounds as directed in master recipe through step 2.

2. While preparing dough, put sausage and ¼ cup water in large skillet. Cook over medium-high heat until water evaporates and sausage cooks through and browns, about 10 minutes. Remove sausage with slotted spoon and set aside. Add enough oil so that amount in skillet equals 1 tablespoon. Add bell pepper and sauté until softened slightly, about 5 minutes. Season with salt and pepper to taste. Set bell pepper aside.

3. Brush oil evenly over each stretched dough round. Spread portion of tomato sauce over each dough round, leaving ½-inch border around edges uncovered. Scatter portion of sausage and bell pepper over sauce onto each dough round.

4. Bake until edges of crusts start to brown, 6 to 12 minutes. Sprinkle with cheese and continue baking until cheese melts, 2 to 3 minutes more. Remove pizzas from oven, cut into wedges, and serve immediately.

▪▪ VARIATION:

Andouille Sausage and Onion Pizza

Substitute andouille sausage removed from casings and broken into bite-size pieces for Italian sausage, replace bell pepper with 2 medium onions sliced thin, and use Spicy No-Cook Tomato Sauce, *see* page 29, in place of tomato sauce with basil.

Figure 24.
*Bulk sausage is easier to incorporate into a pizza topping.
However, link sausage, including sweet or hot Italian sausage,
andouille sausage, or chorizo, will work if you follow these steps.
First, run a sharp paring knife along the length of each link to
slit open the casing.*

Figure 25.
Peel back the casing and remove the meat. Break the meat into
bite-size pieces with your hands.

White Pizza with
Spinach and Ricotta

➤ NOTE: *Ricotta cheese and garlicky sautéed spinach flavor this tomato-less pizza.*

1	recipe Thin-Crust Pizza (*see* page 33)
2	tablespoons olive oil, plus extra for brushing on stretched dough
4	medium garlic cloves, slivered
¼	teaspoon hot red pepper flakes
1¼	pounds spinach, stemmed, washed, partially dried, and chopped coarse
	Salt and ground black pepper
1	cup ricotta cheese
¼	cup grated Parmesan cheese

▦ INSTRUCTIONS:

1. Prepare dough rounds as directed in master recipe through step 2.

2. While preparing dough, heat 2 tablespoons oil in deep saucepan set over medium heat. Add garlic and pepper flakes and cook until fragrant, about 1 minute. Add damp spinach, cover, and cook, stirring occasionally, until just wilted, about 2 minutes. Season with salt and pepper to taste. Transfer to bowl with slotted spoon, leaving behind any liquid. Set spinach aside.

3. Brush oil evenly over each stretched dough round. Arrange portion of spinach over each dough round, leaving ½-inch border around edges uncovered. Dot with ricotta and sprinkle with Parmesan.

4. Bake until edges of crusts brown, 6 to 12 minutes. Remove pizzas from oven, cut into wedges, and serve immediately.

White Clam Pizza

➤ NOTE: *This pizza is a specialty of New Haven, one of the great pizza capitals of America. Traditionally, freshly shucked clams are tossed with garlic, olive, and herbs. Canned clams work as well.*

1	recipe Thin-Crust Pizza (*see* page 33)
2	tablespoons extra-virgin olive oil, plus extra for brushing on stretched dough
6	medium garlic cloves, minced
1	medium onion, minced
½	teaspoon hot red pepper flakes
2	10-ounce cans baby clams, drained, or 24 little-neck clams, shucked
1	tablespoon fresh thyme or oregano leaves
	Salt and ground black pepper
½	cup grated Parmesan cheese

▚ INSTRUCTIONS:

1. Prepare dough rounds as directed in master recipe through step 2.

2. While preparing dough, heat 2 tablespoons oil in large skillet set over medium heat. Add garlic, onion, and pepper flakes and cook until softened and fragrant, 1½ minutes. Stir in clams and thyme or oregano. Season with salt and pepper to taste. Set sauce aside.

3. Brush oil evenly over each stretched dough round. Spread portion of sauce over each dough round, leaving ½-inch border around edges uncovered. Sprinkle with cheese.

4. Bake until edges of crusts brown, 5 to 10 minutes. Remove pizzas from oven, cut into wedges, and serve immediately.

VARIATION:

Red Clam Pizza

Brush oil over dough round. Cover each dough round with portion of Spicy No-Cook Tomato Sauce, leaving ½-inch border around edges uncovered and using 1½ cups sauce in total. Scatter clam sauce over tomato sauce and sprinkle with cheese. Increase baking time by several minutes.

chapter four

DEEP-DISH PIZZA

EEP-DISH PIZZA, PILED HIGH WITH TOMATO sauce, cheese, and toppings, presents several challenges for the home cook. With so much topping, there is a danger of the crust becoming soggy. In our testing, we uncovered several tricks for keeping the crust soft but not soggy.

The first issue, of course, is what kind of pan works best. We tried baking sheets, perforated pizza pans, and round metal pans made especially for deep-dish pizza. We prefer the latter. Dough can be pushed down into the holes in a perforated pan, making the baked crust hard to remove. Baking sheets are not deep enough. We recommend a four-

62

teen-inch round pizza pan that is two inches deep for the recipes in this chapter. We tested shiny and dark pans, and both browned the crust equally well.

When fitting the dough into the pan, build up a lip around the edge of the crust to keep the sauce and other toppings from oozing underneath the dough. We also found it helpful to bake the pizza crust without any toppings for several minutes. Baking the crust until it is set makes it less likely to absorb juices from the tomato sauce or vegetables. To keep the dough from bubbling as it bakes without toppings, simply prick it with a fork.

While thin-crust and grilled pizzas respond to high heat, a thick pan pizza needs time to cook through. If the oven temperature is too high, the crust will burn before the toppings are really hot or the center of the dough is cooked. We found an oven temperature of 400 degrees is perfect. Baking the pizza in the lower third of the oven promotes even browning of the bottom crust. For an even darker crust, bake the pan pizza on preheated quarry tiles or a pizza stone.

The resulting pizza will be about one and one-quarter inches high around the edges and about three-quarters inch deep in the center. Deep-dish pizza is breadier and saucier (use a fork and knife) than thin-crust pizza. A fourteen-inch pizza will feed four as a main course, six if feeding kids and adults.

♔

Master Recipe

Deep-Dish Pizza

➤ NOTE: *Because the dough recipe for pan pizza uses less flour than other recipes, we suggest kneading the dough by hand or in a food processor. This smaller amount of dough can get lost in a big standing mixer. See figures 26–30, page 66, for information on shaping and baking deep-dish pizza.*

1 recipe Deep-Dish Pizza Dough
(*see* page 19)
Olive oil for brushing on pan and dough
and coating hands
Toppings of choice (*see* following recipes)

Master Instructions

1. Prepare dough as directed in pizza recipe. Adjust rack to middle-low position and preheat oven to 400 degrees. Brush about ½ tablespoon oil over bottom and sides of 14-inch pizza pan that measures 2 inches deep. Turn punched-down dough directly into greased pan.

2. Oil hands and press dough with fingertips to fit evenly into pan. While pressing dough, build up 2-inch-high lip around edges of pan. Let dough rest 5 to 10 minutes, during which time lip will fall a bit. With oiled hands, build up lip once again. When pizza goes into oven, lip should be about 1 inch high. The rest of dough should have even thickness of about ¼ inch.

3. Prick dough all over with fork and bake without toppings in preheated oven until crust is set, about 4 minutes. Remove pan from oven. Brush crust with 1 tablespoon oil, prick any bubbles with fork, and add toppings as directed in specific recipes.

4. Return pizza to oven and bake until bottom of crust is lightly browned and toppings are sizzling, 30 to 40 minutes. Remove pizza from oven, and serve immediately.

Figure 26.
Turn the punched-down dough directly into a greased 14-inch
pizza pan. Oil your hands and press the dough with your
fingertips to fit it evenly into the pan.

Figure 27.
While pressing the dough, it is important to build up a lip
around the edge of the pan that will keep the sauce and other
toppings from oozing under the dough. Build up a 2-inch-high
lip, allow the dough to rest for 5 or 10 minutes (the lip will fall),
then build up the lip again. When the pizza goes into the oven,
the lip should be about 1 inch high.

Figure 28.

Prick the dough all over and then bake it without the toppings until the crust is set. Setting the crust before adding the toppings prevents sogginess that would otherwise be caused by moist ingredients like tomato sauce.

Figure 29.

When the dough is set, remove the pan from the oven and brush the crust with 1 tablespoon of oil. If the crust has bubbled, prick it with a fork. Spread the tomato sauce and toppings up to the edge of the lip. Return the pizza to the oven to finish baking.

67

Figure 30.
To see if the pizza is cooked through, lift the crust up with a spatula and check to see if the bottom of the crust is lightly browned. The toppings should also be sizzling before removing the pizza from the oven.

Classic Deep-Dish Pizza
with Tomato Sauce and Mozzarella

1   recipe Deep-Dish Pizza (*see* page 64)
Olive oil for brushing on pan and dough and
coating hands

2   cups Thick Tomato Sauce (*see* page 29)

6   ounces mozzarella cheese, shredded
(about 1½ cups)

INSTRUCTIONS:

1. Fit dough into pan as directed in master recipe through
step 2.

2. Prick dough all over with fork and bake without toppings
in preheated oven until set, about 4 minutes. Remove pan
from oven. Brush crust with 1 tablespoon oil. Spread tomato sauce evenly over crust up to edge of lip.

3. Return pizza to oven and bake until crust is lightly
browned around edges, about 20 minutes.

4. Remove pan from oven and sprinkle cheese over tomato
sauce. Return pizza to oven and bake until cheese is melted
and bottom of crust is lightly browned, 10 to 15 minutes.
Remove pizza from oven and serve immediately.

Deep-Dish Pizza
with Sausage and Mushrooms

➤ **NOTE:** *If you want to use link sausage, see figures 24 and 25, page 56, for information about removing the meat from the casings.*

1	recipe Deep-Dish Pizza (*see* page 64)
¾	pound bulk sweet or hot Italian sausage, broken into bite-size pieces
1½	tablespoons olive oil (approximately), plus extra for brushing on pan and dough and coating hands
1	pound white button mushrooms, trimmed and sliced thin
	Salt and ground black pepper
2	cups Thick Tomato Sauce (*see* page 29)
6	ounces mozzarella cheese, shredded (about 1½ cups)

⠿ INSTRUCTIONS:

1. Fit dough into pan as directed in master recipe through step 2.

2. While preparing dough, put sausage and ¼ cup water in large skillet. Cook over medium-high heat until water evaporates and sausage cooks through and browns, about 10 minutes. Remove sausage with slotted spoon and set aside. Add enough oil so that amount in skillet equals 2 tablespoons. Add mushrooms and sauté until golden brown and juices they release have evaporated, about 7 minutes. Season with salt and pepper to taste. Set mushrooms aside.

3. Prick dough all over with fork and bake without toppings in preheated oven until set, about 4 minutes. Remove pan from oven. Brush crust with 1 tablespoon oil. Spread tomato sauce evenly over crust up to edge of lip. Arrange sausage and then mushrooms over sauce.

4. Return pizza to oven and bake until crust is lightly browned around edges, about 30 minutes.

5. Remove pan from oven and sprinkle cheese over toppings. Return pizza to oven and bake until cheese is melted and bottom of crust is lightly browned, about 8 minutes. Remove pizza from oven, cut into wedges, and serve immediately.

Deep-Dish Pizza with Broccoli, Ricotta, and Mozzarella

➤ **NOTE:** *The broccoli can dry out if added too early during the baking process. Therefore, bake the dough without toppings until it is well set (about ten minutes), then add the broccoli. The cheese is added with the broccoli to keep the florets from burning.*

1	recipe Deep-Dish Pizza (*see* page 64)
2	pounds broccoli, stalks discarded and florets cut into bite-size pieces (about 8 cups)
3	tablespoons extra-virgin olive oil, plus extra for brushing on pan and dough and coating hands
2	medium garlic cloves, slivered
½	teaspoon hot red pepper flakes, or to taste
	Salt
1½	cups ricotta cheese
4	ounces mozzarella cheese, shredded (about 1 cup)

⸬ INSTRUCTIONS:

1. Fit dough into pan as directed in master recipe through step 2.

2. While preparing dough, steam broccoli until tender, about 5 minutes. Heat 3 tablespoons oil in large skillet set over medium heat. Add garlic and pepper flakes and cook until fragrant, about 1 minute. Add broccoli and cook, stirring to coat with oil, for 1 minute. Season with salt to taste. Set broccoli aside.

3. Prick dough all over with fork and bake without toppings in preheated oven until well set and beginning to brown, about 10 minutes. Remove pan from oven. If dough has swollen, prick with fork. Brush crust with 1 tablespoon oil. Spread ricotta evenly over crust up to edge of lip. Arrange broccoli over ricotta and sprinkle with mozzarella.

4. Return pizza to oven and bake until cheese is browned and bubbling and bottom of crust is lightly browned, about 30 minutes. Remove pizza from oven, cut into wedges, and serve immediately.

Deep-Dish Pizza
with Roasted Vegetables

➤ NOTE: *Eggplant, zucchini, squash, and bell peppers are roasted with garlic and thyme and then layered into a deep-dish pie with tomato sauce and mozzarella.*

1	recipe Deep-Dish Pizza (*see* page 64)
1	medium eggplant (about ½ pound), cut crosswise into ¼-inch-thick rounds
2	small zucchini (about ½ pound), halved and cut lengthwise into ¼-inch-thick slices
2	small yellow squash (about ½ pound), halved and cut lengthwise into ¼-inch-thick slices
2	red, yellow, or orange bell peppers (about 1 pound), cored, seeded, and cut into ½-inch-wide strips
8	medium garlic cloves, halved lengthwise
2	tablespoons fresh thyme leaves
4	tablespoons extra-virgin olive oil, plus extra for brushing on pan and dough and coating hands Salt and ground black pepper
1½	cups Thick Tomato Sauce (*see* page 29)
4	ounces provolone cheese, grated (about 1 cup)

:: INSTRUCTIONS:

1. Fit dough into pan as directed in master recipe through step 2.

2. While preparing dough, preheat oven to 450 degrees. Toss vegetables, garlic, and 1 tablespoon thyme with 4 tablespoons oil. Season vegetables with salt and pepper to taste. Spread vegetables out over large baking sheet. Roast until tender, about 20 minutes. Set aside. Reduce oven temperature to 400 degrees.

3. Prick dough all over with fork and bake without toppings in preheated oven until set, about 4 minutes. Remove pan from oven. Brush crust with 1 tablespoon oil. Spread tomato sauce evenly over crust up to edge of lip. Arrange roasted vegetables over sauce.

4. Return pizza to oven and bake until crust is lightly browned around edges, 30 to 35 minutes.

5. Remove pan from oven and sprinkle cheese and remaining 1 tablespoon thyme over toppings. Return pizza to oven and bake until cheese is melted and bottom of crust is lightly browned, about 8 minutes. Remove pizza from oven, cut into wedges, and serve immediately.

chapter five

❧

GRILLED PIZZA

I F YOU THINK GRILLED PIZZA SOUNDS LIKE ONE OF those silly chef-inspired creations, think again. Grilling flatbreads over coals has a long history in Italy. As is our custom in this country, we have made this dish our own by adding distinctly American toppings.

There are a couple points to keep in mind when grilling pizza. Toppings have only a few minutes to heat through (any longer and the bottom crust will burn), so they must be kept fairly light. Therefore, we like to get as much flavor from the crust as possible and recommend the Garlic-Herb Pizza Dough. This dough is so flavorful, we often just brush it with olive oil and serve it as an accompaniment to summer meals. Plain dough will also work fine on the grill.

In our testing, we found that larger crusts are hard to flip, so we recommend small pizzas only for the grill. This necessitates working in batches, so consider grilling pizzas for an informal meal when everyone is gathered in the backyard. As each pizza comes off the grill, serve it immediately. An extra pair of hands to top crusts while you tend the grill is helpful.

If you prefer not to be grilling pizzas to order, the crusts can be grilled until nicely browned on both sides and then slid onto a baking sheet, cooled, covered, and kept at room temperature for several hours. When you are ready to serve the pizzas, brush the top of the grilled pizza rounds with a little oil, add the toppings, and slide the crusts under a preheated broiler for several minutes. While the smoky grill flavor is not quite as intense, this do-ahead method is much easier.

The recipes in this chapter will serve four as a light summer meal (two small pizzas per person) or eight as a first course. Keep the following tips in mind when making grilled pizza.

FLOUR ALL SURFACES. Because grilled pizzas are flipped (the bottom of the dough round eventually becomes the top of the pizza), we do not dust peels (use metal only; wooden peels should not go near the grill) or baking sheets with sandy semolina or cornmeal. Flour will keep the dough from sticking yet will not make the crust gritty.

■■ KEEP TOPPINGS LIGHT AND DRY. Heavy toppings or liquidy sauces will make grilled pizza soggy and should thus be avoided. Raw ingredients that need only be heated through (fresh tomatoes, cheese, sliced shrimp) or cooked ingredients that are fairly dry (sautéed onions, grilled mushrooms or eggplant) are best for grilled pizzas.

■■ BRUSH DOUGH WITH OIL. Oil will help keep grilled pizza dough moist, prevent sticking to the grill, and promote even browning. Keep a brush and small bowl of olive oil nearby when grilling pizzas.

■■ USE LONG-HANDLED TONGS TO FLIP DOUGH. Although we prefer to top grilled pizzas on a baking sheet and not on the grill, your hands will still spend a fair amount of time near the fire. To keep them comfortable, use tongs with long, heat-resistant handles to maneuver the dough.

■■ COVER PIZZA TO HEAT TOPPINGS THROUGH. Use either the grill cover or small disposable pie pans to concentrate heat and get the toppings hot by the time the bottom crust is nicely browned. If the toppings are not ready and the bottom crust is done, you can slide the pizzas onto a baking sheet and run them under the broiler.

Master Recipe

Grilled Pizza

➤ NOTE: *See figures 31–38, page 82, for more information on handling the dough on the grill. See figures 10–15, page 37, for more information on shaping the dough.*

To make pizza in advance, grill dough rounds until both sides are crisp and nicely browned, 2 to 3 minutes per side. Repeat with remaining dough rounds. (Grilled dough rounds can be covered and stored at room temperature for up to 6 hours.) When ready to serve, preheat broiler. Brush tops of grilled dough with oil and add toppings, leaving 1/2-inch border around edges uncovered. Broil until toppings are hot and cheese melts, about 2 minutes. Serve immediately.

1	recipe Garlic-Herb Pizza Dough (*see* page 19)
	Flour for dusting hands, work surfaces, and baking sheets or metal peels
¼	cup extra-virgin olive oil for brushing on dough
	Salt

👑

Master Instructions
Grilled Pizza

1. Prepare dough as directed in dough recipe. Light grill. Turn punched-down dough out onto lightly floured work surface. Use chef's knife or dough scraper to cut dough into eighths. Form each piece into ball and cover with damp cloth. Let dough relax at least 5 minutes but not more than 30 minutes.

2. Working with one piece of dough at a time and keeping others covered, flatten ball into disk using palm of hand. Starting at center and working outward, use fingertips to press dough to about ½-inch thick. Use one hand to hold dough in place and other hand to stretch dough outward; rotate dough quarter turn and stretch again. Repeat turning and stretching until dough will not stretch any further. Let dough relax 5 minutes, then continue stretching until it has reached diameter of 7 or 8 inches. Dough should be about ¼ inch thick. Use palm to flatten edge of dough. Transfer dough rounds to baking sheets or metal peels that have been lightly dusted with flour.

Master Instructions

3. Check to make sure grill is medium-hot. Brush oil evenly over each stretched dough round and sprinkle with salt to taste.

4. Grill dough, oiled side down, until dark brown grill marks appear, 1 to 2 minutes. Prick any bubbles that develop on top surface. Brush tops with more oil, then flip with long-handled tongs onto clean baking sheet or peel, grilled side up. (If grilling bread without toppings, simply brush tops with oil and flip back onto grill.)

5. Brush grilled dough surfaces with oil and add toppings, leaving ½-inch border around edges uncovered. Slide pizzas back onto grill. Cover and grill until pizza bottoms are crisp and browned, toppings are hot, and cheese melts, 2 to 3 minutes; serve immediately and repeat with remaining rounds.

Figure 31.
Smaller dough rounds are easier to work with when grilling; stretch
the dough on a floured work surface into 7- or 8-inch rounds.
Transfer the stretched dough rounds to rimless baking sheets dusted
with flour. Do not use semolina or cornmeal because the bottom of
the dough will eventually be flipped and covered with toppings.

Figure 32.
Grilling pizza requires a medium-hot fire that will cook the
crust quickly without burning it. To test the temperature, put
your hand 5 inches above the grill surface. If you can hold it
there for 3 or 4 seconds, your fire is the right temperature.

82

Figure 33.
When the fire is ready, brush the tops of the dough rounds with
oil and sprinkle them with salt. Slide your hand under each
dough round and gently flip the dough onto the grill, oiled side
down. Cook them until dark grill marks appear, 1 to 2 minutes.

8 3

Figure 34.
Use a knife or fork to prick any bubbles that develop on the surface.

Figure 35.
Brush the tops with more oil, then flip the rounds with long-handled tongs onto a clean baking sheet, oiled side down. (We find that topping the pizzas right on the grill can be difficult given the intense heat and thus prefer this method.)

8 4

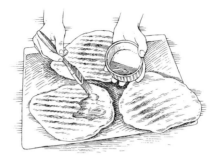

Figure 36.
Brush the grilled surface, which is now facing up, with more oil.

Figure 37.
*Quickly arrange the toppings over the grilled surface, leaving a
½-inch border around the edges uncovered.*

85

Figure 38.
Slide the pizzas back onto the grill. Cover and grill them until
the pizza bottoms are crisp and browned, 2 to 3 minutes.
If you are working with a lot of pizzas, it may be easier to top
one, slide it back on the grill, and then cover it with a disposable
aluminum pie pan while brushing and topping the next pizza.
This method also comes in handy when grilling over an open fire.

86

Grilled Pizza with Fresh Tomatoes and Basil

➤ **NOTE:** *When tomatoes are at their best and all your cooking is outside on the grill, think of this light pizza, which makes a good lunch for four or a first course for eight.*

1	recipe Grilled Pizza (*see* page 79)
¼	cup extra-virgin olive oil
3	medium ripe tomatoes (about 1 pound), cored and sliced crosswise into thin rounds
½	cup grated Parmesan cheese (optional)
1	cup lightly packed chopped fresh basil leaves Salt and ground black pepper
¼	cup pitted and quartered oil-cured black olives

INSTRUCTIONS:

1. Grill dough rounds as directed in master recipe through step 4.

2. Brush grilled dough surfaces some oil. Arrange portion of tomatoes over each dough round, leaving ½-inch border around edges uncovered. Sprinkle with optional Parmesan, basil, and salt and pepper to taste. Drizzle with remaining oil and dot with olives if using.

3. Continue grilling pizzas, covered, until topping is hot and cheese melts, 2 to 3 minutes. Serve immediately.

Grilled Pizza with Shrimp and Feta Cheese

➤ NOTE: *This pizza is moister than some of the others and works well as a dinner for four when served with a salad.*

1	recipe Grilled Pizza (*see* page 79)
¼	cup extra-virgin olive oil, plus extra for brushing on stretched dough
6	medium garlic cloves, minced
4	teaspoons minced fresh oregano leaves
	Salt and ground black pepper
1	pound medium shrimp, peeled and halved lengthwise (*see* figure 39)
8	ounces feta cheese, crumbled (2 cups)

INSTRUCTIONS:

1. Prepare dough rounds as directed in master recipe through step 2.

2. While preparing dough, combine ¼ cup oil, garlic, 2 teaspoons oregano, and salt and pepper to taste in small bowl. Set herb oil aside.

3. Check grill heat and brush plain olive oil evenly over each stretched dough round. Grill, oiled side down, until dark brown grill marks appear, 1 to 2 minutes. Brush tops with more plain olive oil, then flip onto clean baking sheet, grilled side up.

4. Arrange portion of shrimp over each dough round, leaving ½-inch border around edges uncovered. Brush some herb oil over each pizza, making sure that shrimp are lightly brushed with oil as well. Sprinkle cheese and remaining 2 teaspoons oregano over shrimp.

5. Continue grilling pizzas, covered, until shrimp are pink and cheese melts, 2 to 3 minutes. Serve immediately.

Figure 39.
Halving the shrimp lengthwise allows them to cook through on top
of the pizza and eliminates the need to precook them.
Peel the shrimp and use a sharp paring knife to cut along the back.
Remove the vein if you like as you separate the halved shrimp.

Grilled Pizza with
Portobello Mushrooms and Onions

➤ NOTE: *You can sauté the onions well in advance, but because you grill the mushrooms, it makes sense to cook them right before grilling the pizzas.*

1	recipe Grilled Pizza (*see* page 79)
¼	cup extra-virgin olive oil, plus extra for brushing on stretched dough
2	medium onions, halved and sliced thin
2	tablespoons balsamic vinegar
1	teaspoon minced fresh oregano or thyme leaves Salt and ground black pepper
4	medium portobello mushrooms (about 1 pound), stems discarded
½	cup grated Parmesan cheese

▉ INSTRUCTIONS:

1. Prepare dough rounds as directed in master recipe through step 2.

2. While preparing dough, heat 2 tablespoons oil in large skillet. Add onions and sauté over medium heat until golden, about 8 minutes. Stir in vinegar and cook until liquid has evaporated, about 1 minute. Stir in oregano or thyme and salt and pepper to taste. Set onions aside.

3. Brush mushrooms with 2 tablespoons oil. Season with salt and pepper to taste and grill, gill sides up, until caps are streaked with dark grill marks, 8 to 10 minutes. Remove mushrooms from grill and cut into ¼-inch strips. Set mushrooms aside.

4. Check grill heat and brush oil evenly over each stretched dough round. Grill, oiled side down, until dark brown grill marks appear, 1 to 2 minutes. Brush tops with more oil, then flip onto clean baking sheet, grilled side up.

5. Brush grilled dough surfaces with oil. Arrange portion of onions and mushrooms over each dough round, leaving ½-inch border around edges uncovered. Sprinkle cheese over vegetables.

6. Continue grilling pizzas, covered, until vegetables are hot and cheese melts, 2 to 3 minutes. Serve immediately.

Grilled Pizza with
Grilled Eggplant and Goat Cheese

➤ **NOTE:** *Thin rounds of eggplant are brushed with a garlicky basil oil, grilled, and then layered over grilled crusts and sprinkled with goat cheese.*

1	recipe Grilled Pizza (*see* page 79)
¼	cup extra-virgin olive oil, plus extra for brushing on stretched dough
6	medium garlic cloves, minced
4	tablespoons minced fresh basil leaves
	Salt and ground black pepper
1	large eggplant (about 1 pound), cut crosswise into ¼-inch-thick rounds
8	ounces goat cheese, crumbled (about 2 cups)

▋▋ INSTRUCTIONS:

1. Prepare dough rounds as directed in master recipe through step 2.

2. While preparing dough, combine ¼ cup oil, garlic, 2 tablespoons basil, and salt and pepper to taste in small bowl. Set herb oil aside.

3. Brush eggplant slices with half of herb oil. Grill, turning once, until flesh is darkly colored, 8 to 10 minutes. Set eggplant aside.

4. Check grill heat and brush plain olive oil evenly over each stretched dough round. Grill, oiled side down, until dark brown grill marks appear, 1 to 2 minutes. Brush tops with more plain olive oil, then flip onto clean baking sheet, grilled side up.

5. Brush grilled dough surfaces with remaining herb oil. Arrange portion of eggplant slices over each dough, leaving ½-inch border around edges uncovered. Sprinkle cheese and remaining 2 tablespoons basil over eggplant.

6. Continue grilling pizzas, covered, until eggplant is hot and cheese melts, 2 to 3 minutes. Serve immediately.

Grilled Pizza with Fennel, Sun-Dried Tomato, and Asiago

➤ **N O T E :** *The sautéed fennel and onion topping can be prepared a day in advance of grilling the pizza. Bring to room temperature before using to top pizza.*

1	recipe Grilled Pizza (*see* page 79)
3	tablespoons extra-virgin olive oil, plus extra for brushing on stretched dough
1	large Spanish onion (about 1 pound), halved and sliced thin
1	medium fennel bulb (about ¾ pound), stems and fronds discarded; halved, cored, and bulb sliced very thin
4	large garlic cloves, minced
1	tablespoon fresh thyme leaves
1	teaspoon fennel seeds
¼	teaspoon hot red pepper flakes
	Salt
½	cup drained and slivered sun-dried tomatoes
½	cup grated Asiago cheese

⁝⁝ I N S T R U C T I O N S :

1. Prepare dough rounds as directed in master recipe through step 2.

2. While preparing dough, heat 3 tablespoons oil in large skillet over medium-high heat. Add onion and fennel and cook, stirring often, until vegetables soften, about 8 minutes. Add garlic and continue cooking 2 minutes. Stir in thyme, fennel seeds, and pepper flakes. Season with salt to taste. Set onion-fennel mixture aside.

3. Check grill heat and brush oil evenly over each stretched dough round. Grill, oiled side down, until dark brown grill marks appear, 1 to 2 minutes. Brush tops with more oil, then flip onto clean baking sheet, grilled side up.

4. Brush grilled dough surfaces with more oil. Arrange portion of onion-fennel mixture over each dough round, leaving ½-inch border around edges uncovered. Sprinkle tomatoes and cheese over vegetables.

5. Continue grilling pizzas, covered, until eggplant is hot and cheese melts, 2 to 3 minutes. Serve immediately.

index